Original title:
The Life Puzzle: Missing One Piece

Copyright © 2025 Creative Arts Management OÜ
All rights reserved.

Author: Elliot Harrison
ISBN HARDBACK: 978-1-80566-003-3
ISBN PAPERBACK: 978-1-80566-298-3

Faint Outlines of Belonging

In a world of bits and bobs,
I seek the piece that fits my tabs.
Like socks that wander, lost from pairs,
They roam the house like clueless stares.

A jigsaw friend in pieces here,
Each laugh a clue, each grin, a cheer.
But when the frame just pops one out,
I shake my head and laugh, no doubt!

Disparate Dreams

A dream of cookies that won't bake,
A quest for cheese, or is it steak?
In mismatched socks, I skip and hop,
Each silly wish could easily flop.

The stars aligned, or so I thought,
But where's that piece? Oh, what a plot!
With every whim that loops around,
I trip on laughter, back to ground.

One Piece Away from Wholeness

I'm one piece away from my grand plan,
But where it went? I just can't scan.
Like missing keys or lost TV remotes,
These pesky gaps bring giggles, not gloats.

My heart's a puzzle, silly and bright,
As I juggle pieces, up in flight.
With every chuckle, every slip,
I find myself on a wobbly trip.

The Quest for Belonging

In crowded rooms, I wear my hat,
With mismatched shoes and a silly spat.
Each friend a piece, quirky and bright,
We laugh and twirl in shared delight.

On treasure hunts for what we lack,
We tell wild tales and run off track.
In the laughter's echo, we find our place,
For missing bits don't steal our grace.

In Search of the Unseen Piece

I lost my piece, it went astray,
Like socks that vanish in the fray.
My jigsaw quest, a comic plight,
To find that rogue in broad daylight.

With magnifying glass, I scan the floor,
Last seen in the kitchen, behind the door.
A cat stares at me, a furry sage,
As I crawl around in this funny cage.

I check the fridge, it's not in there,
Perhaps it's hiding with my lost pair?
Under the couch, oh what a mess,
Puzzles and crumbs, pure happiness!

And finally, it's stuck in my shoe,
Oh, the irony, who knew it flew?
One small piece, yet such a spree,
Turns life's laughter into sweet misery.

Beyond the Fragments We Know

A thousand bits laid out in glee,
Yet one small square eludes me!
I've searched high and low, even the cat,
Why can't we find that one silly mat?

It might be in the toaster, I reckon,
Or doing the tango with old chicken.
Under the sofa, it might laugh and tease,
Hiding with dust bunnies, oh if you please!

In the freezer, I find a surprise,
Not the piece but frozen fries.
Each bit of the puzzle brings joy and cheer,
But without that one, it's like evil in sheer!

With friends I laugh, we take a break,
Let's not get lost over a mistake.
For in this chaos, hey, what a mess,
Missing pieces or love, I must confess!

Navigating the Missing Edge

I set sail on seas of confusion,
In search of my piece, it's a fun illusion.
With a map drawn in crayons, I glide,
Through wildernesses where puzzles abide.

I found a corner, what a delight,
But my missing piece still stays out of sight.
I braced the wilds, fought off the dust,
Found some old shoes, but not a single crust!

In the drawer, I made a grand find,
Old receipts and a sandwich, oh how kind!
A treasure trove, yet something feels wrong,
Where's my lost piece? I search all along.

Finally, I trip, it's under my feet,
A journey absurd, but oh, so sweet!
With laughter echoing, I claim my prize,
Life's funny bits are the best surprise!

A Canvas Longing for Color

My canvas sits in silence, so bare,
A splash of paint is all it could bear.
The sky in gray just won't do,
Yet here I am with a brush that's blue!

A rainbow waits beyond my reach,
But my palette hides what it won't teach.
With every stroke, my dreams collide,
Yet I'm stuck here, with ego as my guide!

Where Shadows Have No Shape

In a world where shadows trip and play,
They dance around in a goofy ballet.
But in my corner, they run amok,
I swear they must be mocking my luck!

A hand tries to grasp what slips away,
A phantom shape that just won't stay.
Am I losing it, or is it a game?
These shadow tricks just smell of a flame!

The Unattainable Corner

In a room with corners all so neat,
I search for that one tiny sheet.
What helps begin my epic tale?
Oh, the frustration that must prevail!

I stack the boxes, I climb so high,
But that sneaky corner just won't comply.
With a wink and a laugh, it taunts my reach,
Just one more step, why can't it teach?

The Intrigue of Incompleteness

A jigsaw piece lies under the bed,
It mocks me daily, fills me with dread.
Bitten off edges of unsolved riddle,
I'll stick it in soup, or maybe a fiddle!

With quirky shapes that twist and turn,
I scratch my head, and yes, I yearn.
But if I find it, what will it prove?
That I'm the champ or I've lost my groove?

Searching for the Final Note

In music's score, a note went stray,
A symphony silent, in disarray.
I searched the attic, looked under the bed,
Found socks and a cat, but not what I said.

Fiddled with buttons, and played with a pen,
Even consulted a wise old hen.
"Cluck once for yes, and twice for no,"
But all she could do was steal the show.

My friends joined in, with a makeshift band,
Made music from spoons, a drum, and a hand.
Laughter erupted, we forgot the chase,
And danced in circles, a wild goose race!

The final note's lost, but here's what I found,
The joy in the journey, a laughter unbound.
With friends around, who needs a tune?
We'll sing to the stars, and howl at the moon!

The Space Between Stars

In the vast cosmos, I've lost a star,
Checked under my pillow, looked near my car.
"Could it be hiding?" I ponder with glee,
In the fridge next to pickles, or stuck in a tree?

I called out to aliens, they laughed and replied,
"We don't have your star, but we've got interstellar fries!"

With a side of space-shakes, I joined in their game,
Who knew that the void could look quite the same?

We built a rocket from old cardboard tubes,
Zoomed past the planets, like a crew of goofball fools.
Misplaced a comet, but never lost cheer,
We laughed through the cosmos, with snacks and a beer!

So if you lose something, don't sweat or fret,
Join the galactic dance, and you'll never regret.
The space between stars is where laughter ignites,
Just don't forget snacks for those starry delights!

Frayed Edges of Serenity

In a comfy chair, I sip my tea,
Yet peace got frayed like my old melee.
My cat just yawned, in a zen-like pose,
While the dog gave chase to the neighbor's hose.

I tried meditation, but my mind took flight,
Thought of pizza toppings, and birds in full flight.
Not to mention the laundry, that's piling up fast,
In the race for serenity, I'm never the last.

The candle lights flickered, then snuffed out with grace,
As my hopes and dreams went up in their place.
But amidst the chaos and comic display,
I burst out laughing, and all worries gave way.

So I'll take the frayed edges, the chaos, the fun,
Finding bliss in the mess, for I'm never outdone.
With each silly moment, I craft a new thread,
In the tapestry of laughter, where worries are shed!

Tapestry of Forgotten Dreams

Once stitched a dream, of flying like birds,
Then realized my fear of pesky old nerds!
They'd shout and they'd cheer, 'Hey look at that guy!'
So I stuck to my couch, and waved them goodbye.

Wove a bright future, with glitter and glue,
But the cat stole my sequins, what else could I do?
With yarn tangled round, like a dance gone awry,
I laughed at the mess, instead of asking why.

I tried to un-weave the madness on cue,
But my bobbin was missing, and that just won't do!
A patchwork rebellion, with colors so loud,
Made my spirit rise, amidst the chaos I vowed.

Through stitches of laughter, a tapestry grows,
In a patchwork of moments, my joy freely flows.
With each thread I discover, forgotten, anew,
In this colorful maze, where dreams all accrue!

A Piece Whispering Home

In a box of lost adventures,
One piece keeps looking for its mate.
It gets cozy with odd socks,
And claims it's destined for great fate.

Cheese and socks, a perfect match,
They dance under the table lamp.
But still, the puzzle waits in vain,
For someone to lend a helping hand.

The cat walks by, gives a wink,
As if to say, 'This piece is mine!'
But each time they start to sync,
The socks just laugh, and woefully pine.

Finally, they take a spin,
And roll around on the old floor.
Who knew this piece would find such friends?
In chaos, it's rich with more galore!

The Edge of Unfinished Tales

On a shelf where stories halt,
A piece of jigsaw feels quite shy.
It lies there dreaming of a plot,
Dreading the day it must comply.

A knight once sought a quest, they swear,
Promised adventures so grand and bold.
But all it does now is sit and stare,
Awaiting tales waiting to be told.

The dragon snores, the princess sighs,
While the missing piece kicks back to chill.
It wonders if it's even wise,
To wish for stories strange and ill.

Yet life's a laugh, a comedy,
With gaps that tell a tale so sweet.
And in this silliness, let it be,
A jiggle of joy beneath your seat!

Landscapes of Loneliness

In the wild fields of solitude,
Lies a piece under a lonesome tree.
Surveying life with a fruity hue,
Wondering what it wants to be.

A squirrel skips, with nuts galore,
Hey, what if we could go outside?
'But without my friends?' it roars,
And in the breeze, it starts to slide.

The sun shines bright, yet it's not quite,
As mischievous clouds gather near.
Reaching out, it grabs a kite,
And wonders if that's just its beer.

Yet in this laugh, there's space to roam,
Where other pieces dare not tread.
Perhaps with joy, it'll find its home,
On fields of dreams, where all are fed!

The Intricacies of Untold Stories

Once a piece from a brighter tale,
It slipped and fell, oh what a sight!
It tried to stand, begin to sail,
But tripped instead on a cat's twilight.

Each night, it spins its wildest dreams,
Of dragons, quests, and bold knights' crush.
But every dawn, alas, it seems,
It waits a bit more in a hopeful hush.

Potatoes tease it, rolling around,
While it longs for a destiny wide.
Yet laughter echoes, definitely found,
In quirky turns when it's misapplied.

In the end, despite its plight,
It joins the madness with a grin.
In puzzles and pieces, laugh outright,
For every crack leads to a win!

Shadows of Inquiry

In a world where socks go stray,
I ponder on things that drift away.
The cat's got one, the dryer's a thief,
Finding odd shoes is my only belief.

I search for the spoon, it vanished again,
Where do they hide, those mischievous men?
The fridge is a mystery, it laughs in my face,
Maybe it's winning this curious race.

A puzzle of items, mismatched and lost,
I'll trade in my sanity, but at what cost?
With a grin, I accept this chaotic spree,
At least there's still chocolate waiting for me.

So I giggle at life's little tricks,
As I wade through this ocean of comic conflicts.
With each missing piece that is swallowed by fate,
I've learned to embrace this topsy-turvy state.

Echoes from a Half-Completed Dream

In the land of dreams, I chase a balloon,
It floats past the fridge with a carefree tune.
But wait, what's that? A wayward sock!
It dances around like a tick-tocking clock.

Half-finished thoughts bounce around my head,
Like a pinball machine, ought to be fed.
The lost chunk of words, oh where have you flown?
I'll find you one day, I'll bring you back home.

Laughter erupts from an unfinished quest,
I gather my thoughts; put them to the test.
Will I find that piece, oh how silly to dream!
Though it's fun to pretend, I hear my heart scream.

So here's to the gaps that make life a sport,
With each loose end, I summon the court.
Holding my breath, I'm swinging for fun,
In this game of missing, I'm never outrun.

A Fragmentary Reflection

Tangled in mirrors, I gaze at my face,
But wait, is that my hair's natural place?
Reflecting the chaos, a weave of delight,
Who knew tangled locks could make me feel bright?

The pieces are scattered, much like my mind,
It's hard to stay focused, it's better unconfined.
With each quirk I find, like a rare little gem,
I chuckle at growth, just don't ask me when.

In my fragmentary state, I wander and play,
Losing myself in each quirky array.
With half-finished thoughts and a wink of delight,
I celebrate my gaps as a beautiful sight.

Finding joy in the silly, the cracked and the bent,
Each lopsided jest is for laughter's ascent.
A puzzle of memes, in my quirky old head,
Let's dance with the missing, let's party instead!

Notes from the Unfinished

With notes on the fridge, my ideas run wild,
Each scratchy reminder, like a playful child.
A carrot for dinner or a pizza delight,
Oh wait, what was that? I just lost my sight!

My recipes gather dust like lost dreams in a drawer,
While I noodle on life, can't recall what's in store.
The puns keep on flipping, they dangle and tease,
If laughter's the goal, I'll do this with ease.

From unfinished tasks to titles untold,
I'm searching for humor, marbles uncontrolled.
A footnote of fun amidst voids in the script,
With blank pages waiting, I'll never be whipped.

In this symphony odd, I'll dance with the fuss,
Godspeed to the missing, it's part of the fuss.
So here's to the notes where the sunshine will gleam,
In the mess of the unfinished, I'll craft my grand dream.

Fragments of Brightness

In a box of socks, a lone glove waits,
Wondering where its match elates.
With each tick-tock of the clock,
It plots its escape from this lonely dock.

A puzzle piece peeks from behind the chair,
Half of a cat, or maybe a bear?
Its destiny calls, oh what a tease,
To find that edge of a jigsaw breeze.

The spoon blends in with forks at dinner,
Telling jokes, but none are a winner.
While plates and cups bubble in cheer,
The missing piece shrieks, "I'm still right here!"

With a wink and a grin, life's antics unfold,
In shades of laughter, bright and bold.
For each quirky part, a story to weave,
In this jumbled tapestry, we believe!

Beyond the Edge of Clarity

In a world of marbles, one rolls away,
Claiming it's off to join a parade.
While crayons rebel and colors collide,
The missing piece giggles, "I'll just hide!"

The remote control, a master of disguise,
Hiding from couch cushions, oh what a surprise!
"Change the channel, no, not that one!"
Shouts the family, as the laugh track runs.

A sock on a mission, travels alone,
Dreaming of beaches, far away from home.
Yet here by the dryer, it plots its escape,
To find the other half, to wear and reshape.

In each little search, a twist of time,
With giggles and hiccups, life's silly rhyme.
For in every gap, a chuckle unfolds,
A hint of hilarity, the mystery molds!

Whispers in the Void

The paperclip whispers, "I'm an origami swan!"
While in the junk drawer, chaos gets drawn.
"Hey, where's my lid?" a container fret,
"Lost in the cosmos, I'm not done yet!"

A pair of shoes, mismatched and bright,
Deciding to dance in the soft moonlight.
"Let's spin in circles, who needs a twin?"
As each takes a step, nowhere to begin.

The scales and the spoons, they form a band,
Playing sweet symphonies, oh isn't it grand?
With forks a-tapping, the kitchen's alive,
As laughter and music help us all thrive.

In cracks of the floor, secrets confer,
Every oddity speaks, with a gentle purr.
For in every puzzle, humor shall roam,
The pieces, though missing, still feel like home!

Seeking the Unseen Link

A cat toy rolls under the couch,
Claiming it's off to "meet" a grouch.
While the vacuum hums its heavy song,
The dust bunnies nod, "We've been here long!"

A water bottle teases, playing coy,
"I'll save the world, then find my boy!"
As lids join forces, creating a pact,
To tackle thirst, that's an old fact.

The clock ticks loudly, "Where's my hand?"
In a quest for time, it makes a stand.
While seconds tumble like playful leaves,
The hours giggle, "Let's roll up our sleeves!"

To seek and to find, a joy that's rare,
In life's little quirks, we dance and share.
For every lost piece, a laugh will emerge,
And from this delight, our spirits will surge!

Fractured Wholeness

In a box labeled 'perfect', I found my sock,
One is rugged, the other? Quite a schlock.
My jigsaw thoughts scattered, yet I wear a grin,
Who needs full pictures when you can simply spin?

Life's like a sandwich, one slice just won't do,
I toast, I butter, then I lose my shoe!
I'm half of a potato, peel me with flair,
Add a spritz of laughter, and joy fills the air.

I chased my own shadow, it ran with a rush,
In the race for 'complete', I tripped on a brush.
But every odd piece fits in this wacky dance,
Embrace the nonsense; give chaos a chance!

With quirks and oddities, the fun won't be lost,
Embrace the mishaps, even at a cost.
For in every misfit or comical throw,
Lies a spark of joy that keeps us aglow.

A Missing Beat in the Melody

Once I thought I'd dance, with rhythm so fine,
But tripped on my toe, now I'm out of line.
My partner is laughing, a tune out of sync,
Yet that silly stumble made us both rethink.

With a drum full of giggles, I bopped with flair,
The music forgot me, but I didn't care.
Off-key serenades, we belt like a dream,
With every wrong note, we add to the theme.

A symphony's perfect! Is that what they say?
But my beat's just as good in its quirky way.
Who needs a sonata, with tempo so sweet,
When chaos can hum, while we dance to the beat?

Laughter's the chorus that lightens each fall,
A missing beat's magic; it unites us all.
So grab your odd pieces, let's play and compose,
For in this wild dance, true melody grows.

The Last Piece Healthily Hidden

I searched high and low for that elusive piece,
Behind couches, under beds, my prayers never cease.
It's the last piece of sanity from my jigsaw great,
Yet it hides in the fridge with my milk and my plate.

A treasure of chaos, yet it gives me a chuckle,
Why's the piece of my puzzle with the pickles that buckle?
Can't find missing brains in the laundry, it seems,
But I'm piecing my life, one sandwich at dreams.

The cats are conspiring, I swear on my hat,
They whisper sweet secrets as I follow their chat.
They laugh while I stumble, embracing the whim,
Every missing puzzle adds spice to my hymn.

So raise a toast to the pieces, all quirky and grand,
Each mismatched fit, like a fractured band.
For the last piece held hostage, what a funny show,
Who needs completion when we've got overflow?

Mosaic of Memories Unearthed

I start with a pebble, a memory neat,
But soon it's a boulder, can't find my own feet.
Each laugh adds a chip, each tear brings a hue,
This mural of life grows, though it's far from true.

A splash of an orange, a pinch of despair,
A sprinkle of joy with a side of my hair.
I paint with what's missing, the colors run wild,
Embroidered with laughter from my inner child.

The frames are all crooked, the colors, they clash,
But who says perfection can't come from a splash?
With moments well captured, a story retold,
In the chaos of life, my mosaic unfolds.

So dance through the mishaps, let the laughter bloom,
In the mess we discover, there's always more room.
For in this grand picture, the missing will shine,
Together with memories, your dance and mine.

Threads of Longing

In the basket, I seek my sock,
Searching high and low, what a shock!
Two are here, but one is gone,
Where'd it go? Write a sad song.

My jigsaw's missing a bright piece,
It's somewhere lost, oh sweet release!
I check the dog, I check the cat,
They wink at me like 'What's up with that?'

Coffee spills on my old white shirt,
I dance and twirl, oh, how it hurt!
The stains could tell a tale or two,
Of mornings wild and moments askew.

A key without a lock to find,
Like love that lingers, but stays blind.
I laugh, I cry, oh what a feat,
Just adding to my missing sheet.

The Fray of Lost Love

He left his hat upon my chair,
But did he leave his heart laid bare?
I trip on memories, oh so vast,
Why can't love be more like a cast?

Her lipstick stains my coffee cup,
A sip of love is just the sup!
She texts me memes that make me grin,
But still I feel I'm stuck within.

We danced to songs by goofy bands,
While laughing tight with clumsy hands.
But now I find, after the fun,
I'm just a puzzle piece on the run!

With socks and ties all mismatched too,
I search for hints, donning a shoe.
Love's like my closet, a crazy spree,
So much to cherish, yet lost at sea!

Puzzles Cast Aside

A thousand pieces on the floor,
I'm searching, kicking – what's in store?
I spot a corner, bright and neat,
But where's the middle? That'd be sweet!

Went to the store for a snack attack,
Instead, I bought another pack.
Of puzzles with bits that don't correlate,
Guess I'll be here to celebrate!

That sandwich I made, oh what a mess,
Did I even get the right address?
With mustard on my shirt instead,
I ponder life while craving bread.

My last sock's lonely, it's quite a sight,
Is it a phantom? A sorry plight?
I grin and laugh at all the fuss,
'Cause life's too short, so let's discuss!

Yearning for the Missing Segment

A piece of cake, so sleek and round,
But oh, my fork won't make a sound.
I scoop and slip, it falls away,
Life's just a game I love to play!

With half a heart, it feels the same,
Two left shoes—now that's a shame.
I trip on love, it's quite a ride,
While searching for what's left inside.

A puzzle's edge, so sharp and bright,
Hiding secrets, what a sight!
But every time I snap away,
I lose a piece—hey, where'd it stray?

So here I sit, with mismatched pairs,
Dreaming where my logic dares.
Life's a giggle, a quirky spree,
With missing bits, we're still so free!

An Open Door to Tomorrow

With every lock there's a key,
But mine has gone on a spree.
It danced with socks in a drawer,
Leaving me wanting much more.

The fridge is bare, the shelf is cracked,
The cat's philosophy is whacked.
I'd travel far to find that part,
But where to look? It's a fine art.

My shoes are mismatched, it's true,
One's a boat, the other's a shoe.
I laugh and trip on my own feet,
Life's a circus, such a treat!

Who knew my brain is a maze?
I wander in a daze for days.
The missing piece still hides away,
I guess I'll laugh my cares astray.

Searching for the Untouched Edge

A jigsaw piece lost in my hair,
I find it now, and I just stare.
Is this a puzzle or just fluff?
Life demands I'm smart, not tough!

With mismatched socks and a wild shirt,
I shuffle through the afternoon dirt.
A coffee stain like a work of art,
Is this the missing piece of my heart?

The neighbor's cat steals my lunch,
He's got the flair, I've got the hunch.
I chase him 'round like a mad fool,
Where's that piece? It's breaking the rule!

A collage of moments stuck on rewind,
The missing bits spin round in my mind.
But laughter lines draw all I need,
In silly quests, I plant the seed.

The Forgotten Edge of Being

In the attic, I found my past,
A sock from '09, it's built to last.
It waved hello, said 'stay a while',
I grinned at the dust and the style.

An unopened box of glittering dreams,
With former plans and forgotten themes.
A recipe for joy went missing too,
But I'll bake happiness anew!

Do I need a map or a telescope?
Both are lost; I'll just use hope.
A kaleidoscope of silly sights,
I'll chase the day through endless nights.

The edges may seem rough and torn,
Yet laughter's sound can be reborn.
So here's to the quirks that keep us whole,
The funny pieces make up the soul.

The Whisper of Missing Pieces

There's a whisper in the empty space,
Where laughter hides, a silly face.
I cracked a joke but lost my punch,
Now I'm just a very vague hunch.

A button fell from my favorite coat,
It drifts like dreams on a little boat.
I search the couch and under the bed,
But often find just crumbs instead.

With each twist and turn, I create a mess,
Life's a puzzle; it's anyone's guess.
But a chuckle here and a giggle there,
Turns that piece into fresh air.

So I'll dance in the gaps, sing out loud,
Making joy my very own crowd.
For each missing piece adds to the fun,
In this quirky game, we've all won!

Whispers of Incomplete Dreams

In a world where socks disappear,
My dreams don't seem quite clear.
I chase the shadows of my thoughts,
But always get tangled in silly knots.

The coffee spills on my bright new shirt,
I might as well have danced in dirt.
With half a plan and a wobbly grin,
I wonder where the fun just went in.

A puzzle piece shaped like a cat,
Just doesn't fit, and that's a fact.
I laugh it off with all my might,
As I search for my lost kite in flight.

Oh, the giggles that fill the air,
As I trample my thoughts, unaware.
Every unfinished dream I see,
Has become a joke, just like me.

Traces of What Remains

I lost my keys in the fridge again,
Wondering how I'll get out, when.
The leftovers wink and giggle too,
As I ponder what I should pursue.

Each puzzle piece with a smirk so sly,
Tells me it's simply a pie in the sky.
Shadow of a donut floats by my head,
As I search for the meaning instead.

The hints of laughter fill my space,
With every misplaced thought I chase.
Like finding shoes with mismatched laces,
Life's a game with silly faces.

In this unfinished game we play,
I might just find the bright array.
With every chuckle, I sway around,
Creating joy in the chaos found.

Jigsaw of Heartache

Oh, a heart with pieces all askew,
Like a puzzle missing more than a few.
Each corner I turn spills out some cheer,
But I keep on falling, tumbling near.

My loneliness wears a zany hat,
As I giggle with a friendly cat.
It swats at my hopes with UFOs,
In this game where nobody knows.

Searching for the parts that don't belong,
I laugh at the notes of a goofy song.
The fridge is laughter, the floor is a beat,
Made for clumsiness, how sweet!

So here's to the heart that can't quite mend,
It dances a jig with no real end.
A funny little mix, a colorful show,
At least I have snacks and a warm elbow.

The Elusive Cornerstone

There's a cornerstone that's rolled away,
Hiding behind a game I play.
Every search just leads to crumbs,
Maybe life just wants more fun!

Each missing bit is a chuckle's song,
As I navigate where I belong.
The cats all chuckle from their beds,
While I trip over thoughts in my head.

I draw maps of where my joy could hide,
But they all laugh and knot inside.
Around I go in silly circles,
As the elusive laughs with sparkles.

In the chaos, there's a silly cheer,
For every giggle conquers fear.
No perfect piece, no perfect clue,
Just funny fails and bumbles too.

A Quest in the Abyss

In a sock drawer, I began to seek,
A lost treasure, so hide and seek.
With crumbs of snacks and dust bunnies galore,
I chuckled, 'Who knew? This quest is a chore!'

I rummaged and fumbled, a sight to behold,
What was I after? My story's untold.
A sandwich, some marbles, and one rubber shoe,
Maybe my piece was just up and flew!

The depths of my pockets, a cavern of dreams,
Coins of the past and old candy themes.
If only my memories could fit in a box,
I'd sort through my chaos, like socks with no socks!

Then came the moment, a glimmer of cheer,
A shiny old button that once seemed so dear.
I laughed in surprise, not quite my lost piece,
But hey, in this quest, I found some release!

Pieces Held in Memory

In a photo album, the smiles reside,
Each snapshot a treasure, a joyful ride.
Yet one face is missing, a ghost on the wall,
Who knew that laughter could vanish so small?

We danced in the kitchen, we sang in the rain,
That piece seems elusive, like driving insane.
I sift through the pages, I shake my head slow,
Has anyone seen them? Where did they go?

My mind's a collage of stories and joy,
But one little face—oh, my heart's tiny ploy.
I searched through the fridge and found yesterday's stew,
I laughed at my fridge, "Are you hiding them too?"

In dreams, they visit with hugs full of glee,
Reminding me gently, it's not just me.
The fun isn't over; it's still in our hearts,
Where pieces of laughter will never depart!

The Void of Silent Longing

In the corner of life, an empty chair sits,
I ponder its absence, and throw childish fits.
A blank spot that's yearning, a quirk in my fate,
I swear it was here, just a minute too late!

The vacuum of silence is loud as a drum,
Where is my buddy? They were such good fun.
A sandwich left out and a soft drink alone,
Wait—did they escape? Were they tired of home?

I often imagine them hiding somewhere,
Up on a cloud or down under a chair.
With laughter echoing, the days don't seem bleak,
This empty chair's secret? It's just to make me peek!

So I toast to the void, to the empty space,
May it welcome the laughter, and fill with grace.
And if they should return, oh what joy it would be,
For even the silence can shout, "Come and see!"

A Canvas Yet to Be Colored

In a box of crayons, the reds and the blues,
A piece of my rainbow seems to have snoozed.
I searched for a purple, a bold, spry surprise,
But all that I found were green things that rise!

Yet my canvas sits waiting, not filled with despair,
I'll paint with my passions, create with some flair.
A splash of hot pink, and a twist of the sun,
Who needs all the pieces when creating is fun?

With laughter I swirl all my colors around,
What's missing is magic, the joy that I've found.
Even in chaos, new shades will ignite,
A masterpiece blooms like stars in the night!

So here's to the colors, the laughs and the cheer,
To the missing piece—well, it's not really here!
In this canvas of life, I'll make it my own,
For every lost piece helps my heart to be grown!

Dance of the Lost Element

In a world of socks all full of holes,
The missing mate starts dancing, oh how it strolls!
One in the dryer, the other in a shoe,
Together they plan their caper, who knew?

With mismatched jigsaw pieces around the floor,
A puzzle half done, but oh, the encore!
The cat steals one, the dog chews a piece,
The dance goes on with such furry increase!

Chasing after crumbs, that's how it goes,
The lost element smiles, and the laughter grows.
Their quirky waltz makes us giggle with cheer,
Finding joy in the chaos, no need for fear!

So let's celebrate all the gaps that we find,
In life's quirky dance, we're never maligned.
With socks that have secrets and puzzles unsolved,
We'll always be laughing as our hearts evolve!

The Thread Weaving Silence

A needle and thread in a silent spree,
Stitching a tale of a lost memory.
The button is missing, the shirt it does lack,
We'll hold it together with some tapes on our back!

In corners of closets, old threads like to play,
They weave tales of socks that have gone astray.
Grandma would frown and say with a huff,
With one little piece, it's just not enough!

But the patches just giggle, with colors so bright,
They dance with each other, a marvelous sight.
Life is a quilt of the odd and the fair,
In the tapestry of silence, we find love everywhere!

So here's to the fabric of life's crazy scheme,
With thread unspooled, we're still part of the dream.
Let's craft our own pattern, with pieces all tossed,
For in every stitch, there is beauty embossed!

Unraveled Threads of Existence

An unwound ball of yarn rolls down the lane,
Every twist and turn is a bit of a pain.
The cat catches shadows, the dog steals a thread,
Unraveled lives are better than dead!

In the chaos of stains and mismatched hues,
The fabric of life displays all the blues.
With coffee stains here and some crumbs over there,
We weave through the mess, pretending we care!

Each thread is a story, both silly and grim,
A scarf with a twist, a hat with a whim.
And those silly sock puppets, they sing out of tune,
They tell all our secrets under the moon!

So let's embrace the flaws, the jumbles and spins,
In this tapestry of life, true joy begins.
With all the threads tangled, nothing to fear,
The beauty of existence is laughing right here!

Glimmers of the Hidden Whole

A missing shovel comes back as a spoon,
Baking a cake with a dash of a tune.
With flour on noses, we giggle and grin,
Creating a feast with a sprinkle of sin!

In each little crack where a piece should fit,
Shines the sparkle of childhood, a bright little bit.
We'll build a tall castle with blocks that won't stack,
Everyone knows it's fine to laugh back!

A map with no treasure is still full of fun,
We'll hunt with our friends, we're all on the run.
With treasure maps drawn in the sand on the shore,
The glimmers of laughter make us want more!

So let's celebrate gaps, the quirks in our days,
With giggles and joy in all of our ways.
For though pieces are missing, we still find a whole,
In the heart of the madness lies our funny soul!

Searching for Lost Harmony

In a room of shoes, I seek that left,
Where did it go? Was it the cat's theft?
The sock hops alone, dreaming of its mate,
A dance of mismatched, oh what a fate!

The guitar's missing a happy old string,
It plays a sour note, oh what a fling!
My coffee's gone cold, my toast went awry,
With every new morning, I'm asking 'why?'

Puzzles abound in this whimsical space,
A sock without partner, a smile on my face,
Chasing lost harmony, I trip on my pride,
A jester's cap worn, in laughter I hide.

So here's to the things that just slip away,
A tickle of joy in the disarray,
Let's chuckle together as we search for the key,
For life's little misfits are waiting for me!

An Unfinished Tapestry

A tapestry woven, but oh what a sight,
One patch is missing, it vanished from light.
I check under cushions, behind the fridge's face,
Saved stitches of laughter, like threads in a race.

Each color a story, a riddle untold,
Without that one piece, it's just threads of old.
The cat sits and ponders my patchwork despair,
Mewls at the weavings that hang in the air.

Grandma's yarn ball has rolled off the shelf,
Now it eats my shoes like a sly little elf,
Threading my way through this crafty charade,
Life's fabric unravels, yet I'm unafraid.

So I'll wrap up the chaos, embrace the odd hue,
This unfinished tapestry, oh what a view!
With laughter entwined in each knot that I make,
Crafting my joy, for happiness' sake!

Shadows of a Missing Link

In the depths of my closet, shadows play peek,
A shoe with no partner, how silly and sleek.
The links of my chain have all gone astray,
I'm left with a puzzle that won't go away.

In a world full of anchors, I float like a leaf,
Where's my other half? Could I jest in grief?
The peanut butter's lonely, the jelly's in tears,
It's a sandwich affair that's gone on for years.

The missing link giggles from behind the door,
Waves at my blunders, shouts "give me more!"
With socks on my head and my shirt on askew,
I'm searching for laughter, not silver or blue.

In a dance of delight, I'll twirl and I'll spin,
Celebrate all that's awkward, let the fun begin!
For life's little shadows can shimmer and sway,
With humor and heart, they teach me to play!

Echoes of a Fragmented Journey

On a journey of echoes, I stumble and skip,
My map's upside down; it's a comical trip.
With shoes on the wrong feet, I laugh at the game,
Each step feels like magic, nothing feels lame.

The breadcrumbs are scattered, they lead me astray,
But what's a great story without some dismay?
The compass is laughing; it spins round and round,
In this scatterbrained world, joy's easily found.

A suitcase of memories, but packed way too tight,
The bits I forgot will make this trip bright.
Between giggles and gasps, I'll stumble with glee,
For the echoes of nonsense are just meant for me.

So here's to the journey, the fun we embrace,
With heartbeats and chuckles, I'll finish the race.
For missing a piece isn't lack, it's a chance,
To dance in the silence, to frolic and prance!

The Key to Forgotten Paths

In a drawer, I found my shoe,
The other one danced, who knew?
Keys jingled, a whistling tune,
I lost my thoughts—guess I'll swoon!

Marbles rolling down the street,
Chasing shadows on my feet,
Maps are easy, but I can't see,
Why all the trees look like me!

Plans were made with great delight,
But I forgot them overnight.
A sandwich left to grow some mold,
Awaits the trophy for the bold!

Lost my car right on the roof,
Puzzled by this funny goof.
But laughter blooms where thoughts are scattered,
Finding joy is what really mattered!

Missing Threads of Memory

Socks in pairs are rare as gold,
One's a fashion statement, bold.
Did I wear them, who can tell?
Maybe I should bid farewell!

A puzzle piece under my bed,
Played hide and seek with my head.
In a blanket, there's a snack,
As I search for my missing track!

Memory's thread is kind of frayed,
Hope it doesn't get displayed.
With puzzle pieces out of sight,
Who knew life could be so light?

Using ketchup as my glue,
Things get messy, that feels true.
But in this jigsaw of today,
Laughing keeps the blues at bay!

Silhouettes of Unfinished Lives

Here I stand, a shadow plays,
With spaghetti hair in wild ways.
Have I eaten breakfast yet?
Pretzels greet me with no regret!

Puzzles hang in mid-air dreams,
Filling blank spots with whipped creams.
A dance of socks, a culinary spin,
Why my tea tastes like a win?

Chasing ghosts with birthday hats,
Find me counting playful bats.
Life's a sketch without a pen,
Artistry of might've been!

I misplaced the map of fun,
But that's okay, I'm on the run.
In the canvas of my plight,
Laughter swirls, my guiding light!

Halos of Dreamt Connections

Woke up dreaming of ice cream,
But my cereal lost its theme.
Clouds wore silly hats today,
And giraffes just pranced away!

Frog in a suit, what a sight,
Hopping madly, feeling bright.
Chasing dreams down rainbow roads,
Where all my petite fears erode.

Lost a chord in melodies,
As I strum with wobbly knees.
A pie in the face, oh dear me,
What could be more fun than glee?

With each giggle, life's a spree,
Join the dance of jubilee.
In this game of smiles and cheer,
Missing pieces just bring near!

A Journey Without Closure

I set out on a quest for bliss,
Only to find my sock amiss.
I've got a map but it's upside down,
Is it the way or the road to town?

I searched the fridge for inspiration,
Found only leftovers – a sad relation.
Thought I'd bake a cake, add some flair,
But flour's a ghost that's no longer there.

So here I wander, lost and spry,
With a sandwich whose lettuce dared to fly.
I laugh at the mess, it's truly absurd,
The quest for joy should come with a word.

Yet with each step, I giggle more,
In this whimsical quest, I can't keep score.
Perhaps the journey's just my decree,
To find incomplete joy is still quite the spree.

Confessions of the Incomplete

Dear diary, today I lost my mind,
Or was it my keys? I'm not quite aligned.
I tried to dance but tripped on my shoe,
Now I'm a meme, it's sadly true.

I bought a puzzle, pieces galore,
But it turns out, I'm missing four.
I keep looking under the couch so neat,
Where else could they hide and still be discreet?

I asked my dog, "Have you seen the bit?"
He just wagged his tail – I'm sure he's a wit.
So I sit with the scattered, laugh at my plight,
In this chaotic dance, there's humor tonight.

Maybe it's fate, I just need to embrace,
That joy is imperfect, and that's not a disgrace.
Give me a laugh, or a friend with glee,
For my incomplete story's better, you see.

The Fragment that Completes

In a world where socks take flight,
I search for a mate, but they're out of sight.
One's a wizard, the other a troll,
Both have escaped and left me with a hole!

I found a piece of a jigsaw fair,
But it's from a picture of a cat in a chair.
What's that doing in my big cake plan?
Did my puzzle piece take a vacation span?

I tried to cook, but burned my toast,
What a culinary treat, I'm not proud to boast.
With smoke alarms dancing, I conjured a grin,
The kitchen may flop, but I'm set to win!

So here's to fragments that make us whole,
To mismatched socks and a humorous stroll.
Life's a patchwork of joy and despair,
And in laughter, we find pieces to share.

Pieces in the Wind

I tossed my confetti, but lost half the stream,
It swirled like a kite, a comical dream.
The balloons all flew, one with a sneer,
As if saying, "Thanks, I'm out of here!"

Chasing marshmallows, they jumped from my cup,
I yelled, "Come back!" but refused to sup.
So I sipped my coffee, with foam on my nose,
What do I do when the pieces oppose?

That ukelele, strumming a tune,
But all I can find is an old rubber shoe.
I laugh and I play with my quirky quest,
In this twisted tale, I feel quite blessed.

So here's to the laughter that fills up the gaps,
In the puzzling life of mismatched mishaps.
With giggles and joy, I'll take any bet,
For missing pieces just make me aset!

A Fragment of Distant Horizons

In a box filled with pieces, I sighed,
One edge was missing, oh, how I tried!
A cat claimed the corner, with pride so grand,
He's part of my jigsaw, not quite what I planned.

The colors are bright, but where is that piece?
It rolled under the couch, is it lost or in Greece?
I've searched every drawer, and peaked 'neath the bed,
My puzzle's a game of "what's wrong with my head?"

A nearby neighbor laughs, says, "You think it's a crime!"
The coffee's gone cold, I've wasted some time.
I'll glue all the bits, make an art piece divine,
Who needs the last piece? This chaos is fine!

So I smile at the mess, embrace every flaw,
Life is just jumbled, and isn't that raw?
With missing connections, I'm all set to roam,
In this quirky adventure, I've found my true home!

The Missing Echo of Yesterday.

I woke up this morning, my puzzle all spread,
But something was off in the space in my head.
That corner I needed, just vanished, poof!
Was it eaten by gremlins who scoffed at my woof?

Hints of last weekend lay scattered around,
A piece might be hiding beneath the merry sound.
With laughter and giggles, my friends made a mess,
I'm convinced one of them is the cause of my stress!

Was it Fred with his chips, or maybe sweet Sue?
She had too much soda, that much is true.
Together we pondered, "Did we hide it in bliss?"
But alas, it seems missing, a hit or a miss!

Now I sit with my shadow, the coffee goes cold,
Waiting for friends to come back, I am told.
A party of laughter, though puzzles don't fit,
Life's pieces are funny; at least, I won't quit!

Fragments of a Whole

Sorting the pieces, I'm hot on the trail,
One squished in my pocket, like it's in jail.
I crack a few jokes as I slip it in place,
Only to find it belongs to a race!

The cat came to help; he jumped on the floor,
Launched my whole puzzle out through the back door.
Now I'm chasing bits, like a wild little dance,
Should I thank him for chaos or blame him my chance?

My friend laughs and says, "Let's make it a game!"
Let's take each odd shape and see if they claim:
A heart or a tree; it's a mystery feast,
With pieces so silly, who knows what's released?

With laughter and jigsaw, we're piecing our fun,
Missing bits scattered like crumbs when we run.
So here's to the fragments that mix in our days,
Life's never all tidy, and that's how we play!

A Single Piece in Silence

I sat in a corner, my puzzle so bright,
But one piece was hiding, it gave me a fright.
I looked up and down; was it here or out there?
Maybe my dog took it, with that guilty stare!

A whimpering echo came from the shelf,
I searched through old books, decided to delve.
A missing connection, it's where all the laughs,
Dance through the air like silly giraffes!

I climbed on a chair, tried to search for the clues,
And ended up stuck; just what could I use?
The cat found the piece, my savior in fluff,
Proudly it pranced, "But this is enough!"

So I glued what I had, embraced the mad mess,
With laughter abounding, I simply confessed:
It's funny, this game, with pieces astray,
Life's quirks come together in their own funny way!

Shattered Reflections

In the mirror, I see a clown,
With mismatched socks and a floppy crown.
I'd dress up sharp if I could find,
That missing shoe, it boggles the mind!

I spilled my coffee, oh what a sight,
On my face, there's a latte fright.
The day feels off, like a joke gone bad,
Could it be the piece that I never had?

My clock is ticking, but it's stuck at three,
I dance to a song that forgot the melody.
Every moment's silly, just out of reach,
Like a penguin trying to fly at the beach!

So here I stand with my lopsided grin,
Searching for joy where the mess begins.
Maybe the laughter is the missing link,
In life's ridiculous puzzle, let's not overthink!

A Quest for the Elusive Piece

With a magnifying glass, I start my quest,
For a piece so sly, it's the ultimate test.
I search in the fridge but only find cheese,
And a couple of leftovers that were meant to please.

I checked my shoes and the pockets of pants,
Hoping that maybe it might take a chance.
But just like a magician, it sneaks from my view,
Could it be hiding with my missing shoe?

The cat gives me a look, like I'm the fool,
He knows where it's hiding, playing it cool.
I bribe him with tuna, what more can I do?
Yet he just turns away, like I'm the dog chew.

In my epic saga, I tumble and roll,
For the piece of the puzzle that's taken its toll.
I'll laugh at the chaos, it's part of the fun,
I might need a map, or maybe just run!

Echoes of Incomplete Stories

Once upon a time, in a land so grand,
Where the stars danced, and dreams were planned.
Yet one little tale never made the cut,
Like a donut with holes that firmly shut.

I built my tower with blocks outta place,
Only to find, there's no outer space.
The rocket's missing, but who needs the thrill?
I'll soar on my broomstick, if only for the chill!

In sketches half-done, my characters pout,
Wishing for endings they can rave about.
I scribble and laugh at this curious plight,
At least I have humor to brighten my night!

So here I sit with my pen in hand,
Creating the tales that were never planned.
Incomplete stories, they just make me grin,
Who needs perfection? Let the fun begin!

Shadows of What Could Be

In the shadowy corners of dreams untold,
Lies a piece that sparkles, daring and bold.
I trip over giggles, they float in the air,
Like bubbles of laughter that disappear where?

The paths I wander are wobbly and wild,
Like a toddler confused, yet still defiled.
For every wrong turn is a joke in disguise,
With llamas on bikes and pies that surprise!

Searching for wisdom in a sock drawer deep,
I find a lost sandwich and some bits of sleep.
It's all just a riddle with punchlines galore,
Could the piece that I seek be a knock at the door?

So I'll dance through the shadows, embrace every flaw,
Each piece of this riddle just adds to the awe.
Life's a grand circus, with clown shoes to wear,
Let's laugh at the missing, and breathe in the air!

Life's Unraveled Threads

In a box of socks, one goes astray,
Left with odd pairs, on laundry day.
Matching madness, a sock's great quest,
Who knew cotton could cause such unrest?

Lost my marbles, where could they be?
Under the couch or stuck in a tree?
Laughter bubbles when you search for clues,
Life's hidden treasures, just old worn shoes!

Every recipe needs a secret spice,
Yet I've got flour, and you've got mice!
Chasing the taste of a perfect pie,
But all I bake is an unholy fry!

In the funhouse mirror, I see a clown,
Life's twists and turns, they spin me around.
But laughter beats sorrow, let's give a cheer,
At least we know we're all a bit weird!

Seeking the Heart of Wholeness

On the road to find my missing shoe,
I tripped on a pebble, that's nothing new!
Hopping on one foot, a dance of despair,
   Maybe I'll find it, up in the air?

Searching for gold, I found tin instead,
A treasure map where logic has fled.
Digging through nonsense, laughter's my gold,
Who knew that missing meant nothing so bold?

With a spoon I tried to scoop up the sun,
But it melted quickly—oh, wasn't that fun!
Chasing reflections that dance on the wall,
Life's silly moments are the best of them all.

Wrapped in a blanket, I sip on my drink,
Why bother with missing? Let's pause and think!
Each silly blunder adds colors, you see,
In this quirky journey, I'll never be free!

The Promise in Missing Links

Tangled in thoughts like spaghetti at night,
I searched for the fork that was lost out of sight.
One noodle's adventure leads to another,
It's a cooking disaster, but what a fun smother!

Puzzle pieces scattered across the floor,
A cat's found the corner, and it's starting to roar.
While I'm busy searching for that last little part,
I find joy in the chaos, it's a true work of art!

Missing a button, my shirt's feeling loose,
Fashion's not fun when you're letting it juice.
But who needs style when you've got a grin?
I'm rocking this look, let the laughter begin!

As I stumble through what life may neglect,
I'll cherish the moments we often reject.
For every misstep is a chance to embrace,
The silly adventures that time can't erase!

The Lost Element of Existence

Looking for answers in a bowl of stew,
I find floating carrots, and maybe a shoe!
Culinary quests can be strange, it's true,
But the flavor of life is a savory brew.

In search of the brightest spark of delight,
I found only socks and a furry delight.
My answers are fuzzy, but aren't we all?
Let's throw a party, and answer the call!

Dancing with shadows that play on the wall,
Every misstep can turn into a brawl.
Yet laughter is magic that fills up the space,
In the gaps of our lives, let joy be the grace.

When I seek perfection, I miss the whole show,
But imperfect moments make time gently flow.
So here's to the snippets that make our hearts hum,
In this wacky existence, let's all be a drum!

In the Absence of Closure

I searched for my sock, it fled in the night,
Leaving me puzzled, in a sockless plight.
The cat, a sly thief, wears it with pride,
While I hop like a rabbit, with nowhere to hide.

The fridge holds my lunch, it's a mystery great,
Moldy with secrets, it tempts me to fate.
A sandwich from Monday, so tired and gray,
I'll cherish its mold like an old cabaret.

The kettle is boiling, and maybe it's mad,
It hisses and steams, this appliance I've had.
Did I add just the right amount of zest?
Now I'm drinking tea while wearing a vest.

The door to my cabinet swings open wide,
Spices dance out like they've got something to hide.
I ponder my choices, a culinary spree,
But all I can find is salt and a pea.

The Unwritten Page

With a pen in my hand, I stared at the sheet,
Blank as a pillow, it laughed at my feat.
Wrote down an idea, then lost it in space,
Now all that remains is a doodle of grace.

My thoughts like a squirrel, they dart here and there,
One's hiding in cupboards, the other in air.
I chase after rhymes, but they giggle and flee,
Leaving me pondering where could they be?

In an attic of dreams, where ideas grow wild,
I find mismatched socks and my inner child.
We laugh at the chaos, together we play,
Creating new stories, just frayed in the fray.

The clock keeps on ticking, my deadline draws near,
But the words are just dancing, too drunk on cheer.
With nonsense I write, it's a jubilant race,
And somehow it's me who's forgetting my place.

Lost in the Hues of Being

Life's a fine painting, with colors all wrong,
Like a rainbow that's shy, afraid to be strong.
I mixed red with green, made a fruit salad stain,
Now my canvas looks less like art, more like rain.

The sun in the morning is a bright, goofy chap,
Pouring down giggles, with a bellyful clap.
While shadows play tag, they tickle my feet,
I stumble in laughter, oh, what a feat!

My friends are like crayons, broke and misused,
Each one a tale, some happy, some bruised.
We gather like pixels in digital glee,
Crafting our stories, both silly and free.

Yet, as nightfall arrives, with a wink and a smile,
I glance at my palette, things get quirky and wild.
In swirls and in splashes, where chaos is king,
Life's hues purely blending leads to colorful zing.

Abyss of Yearning

I look in the fridge for a snack or a bite,
But all that is lurking is leftover fright.
A moldy-old pizza giggles at me,
In the abyss of longing, it's not meant to be.

I stare at the sky, wishing on stars,
But they twinkle at me like they know my scars.
Each wish that I make seems to fizzle away,
Leaving me hungry with nothing to say.

My heart yearns for chocolate, my head shouts for cake,
But the diet I chose is a big silly fake.
I dream of sweet frosting with sprinkles on top,
Yet here I am munching on a sad carrot flop.

In the depths of desire, I dance through the night,
With a spoon in my hand, I prepare for a fight.
For in every longing, there's laughter and cheer,
And a scoop of good humor can banish the fear.

A Solitary Piece of Solitude

In a box, I sit alone,
Wondering where I might have flown.
A corner piece, they say I lack,
Wishing I had my friends back.

The table's bare, oh what a sight,
They laugh and say it's quite a plight.
Keep searching here, look under chairs,
Perhaps I've joined the missing flares!

My shape is odd, my color bright,
Pretend I'm cool, but it's not right.
With each new dash, it's less of fun,
Feeling like half the song is done.

Yet still I chuckle, can't complain,
Life's a game, despite the pain.
One day they'll find me, that's the goal,
Until then, I'm a rogue in a hole.

Unraveled Connections

A piece here, a piece there,
Trying to fit in this wild affair.
Came with intent to charm the crew,
But my edges just don't seem to do!

Two pieces laugh, they make a show,
While I just sit like, 'Where'd they go?'
I twist and turn, a tangled mess,
Are friends just a state of guess?

I tried to fit in with the big ones,
But here I am, still having fun.
Maybe I'm meant to dance alone,
On shelves of laughter, I have grown!

So I embrace this joyful gap,
Fill it with jokes, maybe a rap.
At least I'm bright, an odd little chap,
Unraveled, but still in the flap!

The Void Between Us

In the box, they say I'm lost,
Missing friends, oh what a cost!
Two edges whisper, building ties,
While I just sit here, spinning lies.

I stretch and reach to touch their side,
But there's this gap—no need to hide!
I told a joke, they laughed in glee,
But couldn't wrap around me, you see?

Stuck in limbo, what can I do?
Organize chaos, that's my cue!
Though I'm absent from the grand design,
I'll throw a party, and it will shine!

So here I roll, a playful twist,
In this void, I'll still exist.
With laughter ringing, I will cope,
For all that counts is a little hope!

A Puzzle with No Picture

No image here to guide my way,
Just pieces scattered, come what may.
A jigsaw without a single hint,
My edges don't fit, oh what a stint!

They piece themselves, I just watch amazed,
While I ponder, feeling quite dazed.
A unicorn's horn, or a cat's lost ear,
What am I doing? My mind's in gear!

They laugh and dance, an artful few,
As I try to join, but can't break through.
Embrace the chaos, they say with a grin,
In this game, let the silliness win!

So here I lie, an odd door hinge,
Still dancing along the quirky fringe.
A puzzle with no picture shown,
Crafting laughter as my throne!

The Journey of Lost Connections

I lost my keys, then found a sock,
My morning coffee's turned to rock.
With every twist, the laughs abound,
A missing link where joy is found.

I texted you, but sent it wrong,
A cat meme meant to sing a song.
We giggle as we share our fate,
Two peas in a pod, though we're late!

A plan was made to meet at three,
But I forgot the time, you see?
Yet in this mess, we still can thrive,
Embracing chaos, feeling alive!

The journey's wild, but oh so sweet,
Each missed connection is a treat.
With every laugh, we stitch the seam,
In this crazy life, we chase the dream.

Cracks in Time's Design

Tick-tock goes the clock, oh dear,
I'm late again, it's crystal clear.
But in this race, I trip and fall,
Laughter echoes down the hall.

A sandwich made from last week's bread,
With a side of thoughts inside my head.
I find the humor in the mess,
Life's quirks are what I love the best!

A mind that wanders, where's the guide?
I'm lost in socks, can't find my pride.
But with a grin, I laugh aloud,
In these silly moments, I'm so proud.

Time's design is full of cracks,
Where laughter lives and never lacks.
So here's to joy in every blunder,
Forget the stress, let's roll in thunder!

An Incomplete Symphony

I tried to play a perfect tune,
But ended up with cats and moon.
Instead of notes, I found a snack,
A symphony of cheese and quack!

My spoons are forks, my beats a mess,
Yet still, I jam with happiness.
With every wrong note, joy takes wing,
In the chaos, hear the laughter ring!

I read the score, but lost my way,
Dancing wildly, come what may.
My incomplete song, a funny ride,
In this wacky space, I wish to glide.

So here's to tunes that twist and shout,
A melody that's full of doubt.
With laughter noted on every line,
In my heart, it's still divine!

Fleeting Echoes of Solitude

In quiet corners, I lose my thoughts,
Oops, there's a cat, oh no, I bought
A garden gnome with a funky hat,
Now he's my friend—how about that?

I wear mismatched socks, what a style!
Embracing chaos with a smile.
In solitude, I often grin,
For every loss, there's fun to win!

Echoes of laughter fill the space,
In my small world, I find my place.
Chasing shadows, I hum a tune,
Making friends with the dust and moon.

So if you find yourself alone,
Just grab a gnome, you'll feel at home.
In fleeting moments of silly glee,
Embrace the joy of being free!

The Gap in the Canvas

In a world full of color, I search for the shade,
My socks don't match, I'm feeling dismayed.
The paint drips down, a drip from my brush,
Did I leave the door open? Oh, what a crush!

A cat in a hat just danced on my desk,
He's truly the king, I'm nothing but a jest.
The colors explode, but where's my bright hue?
I mixed up the paints, and now I'm quite blue.

A canvas so big, with a hole in the side,
I tried to create, but my talent just died.
I'll stick to my daydreams and leave art to the pros,
Though my cat thinks I'm splendid, I guess he just knows!

A missing piece here, a quirky twist there,
My masterpiece shrinks, but I don't have a care.
I'm laughing at chaos, a giggle from fate,
So let's sip some tea and just celebrate.

Interstellar Yearning

In a spaceship lost, I found a green sock,
My GPS failed, oh what a shock!
Stars in all colors, but none come in pairs,
And what is that smell? Is it cosmic affairs?

I asked a space alien where I should go,
He offered me pizza and said, 'Take it slow!'
With stardust on my nose and joy on my mind,
I traveled through space, leaving worries behind.

But wait, what's this gap in my rusted old ship?
Did I forget a piece? Oh, give me a tip!
An asteroid belt dances, it's quite the fine sight,
But I'm just wishing for socks that are tight.

With planets for pillows, and moons made of cheese,
I hitchhiked on comets, all floated with ease.
But if I can't find my socks, I might just combust,
So send me some laundry, oh universe, please!

The Puzzle's Heartbeat

There once was a puzzle, jumbled and wide,
With pieces that giggled, oh what a ride!
I flipped them and turned them, made faces in play,
And laughed at the corners that wouldn't obey.

Each piece held a story, a place and a time,
But one little part was mysteriously prime.
I searched in the fridge, and under the couch,
A quest for that piece, like an over-hyped vouch!

I found a grumpy llama just munching my rug,
"Excuse me!" I said, "Please don't be a thug!"
I offered him treats, and he pointed his nose,
To a piece hiding out where no one else goes!

With laughter a-plenty, I fixed up the frame,
My puzzle was done, though it's slightly insane.
And the llama just grinned, with a wink and a nod,
My masterpiece sparkled, oh how it was flawed!

Solitude's Silent Space

In my quiet nook, with a book on my lap,
I searched for a thought—a whimsical map.
But my mind went wandering, took off like a kite,
And I couldn't find it, no matter how bright!

A teacup and cookie sat waiting for me,
While I pondered the great cosmic mystery.
But my chocolate chip fell! Oh no, what a fate,
Now I'm scraping crumbs—life's a wonderful state!

I scribbled and doodled, but nothing made sense,
Just tall tales of turtles and time travel suspense.
With a giggle I realized what humor can bring,
When solitude's shadows make laughter take wing.

So here in my fortress, devoid of a chain,
I'll sing to the silence, for that's my domain.
With laughter in my heart, I'll dance to my tune,
For missing a piece is just part of the boon!

www.ingramcontent.com/pod-product-compliance
Lightning Source LLC
Chambersburg PA
CBHW051633160426
43209CB00004B/633